THE PAINLESS PASSOVER

Haven't we all been there done that with those long humdrum Seders? How many times do we need to ask those four questions and point to food on a plate? Every year on Passover we spend many hours at our Seder doing these traditions. For some they may ask a fifth question … *"Can't we just let Passover, pass over"?*

For the first time ever there is a Seder that comes to life! It's called, *The Painless Passover*! It was written with humor yet with a profound touch. There is no more trying to figure out what page everybody is on. It is easy to follow without losing any of the integrity that a traditional Haggadah follows. It provides answers to the symbolic meaning of the holiday of Passover.   No matter whom your guests are, no matter what age, religion or background they come from, *The Painless Passover* will be enjoyed and remembered.

The Painless Passover … is a little treasure book. It will bring you many years of the best Passovers Seders ever! Enjoy and Chag Sameach!

D1365405

ROLES FOR THE SEDER SERVICE

NARRATOR:

This role should be assigned to the most lively and animated person. (This role has a lot of speaking parts.)

THE DEMONSTRATER:

This role is a non-speaking part. This is the person who will be actively showing and pointing to the things on the Seder table for the guests to see.

MAN OF THE HOUSE:

This is a role is for the head of the household who usually leads the Seder service. It has a lot of speaking parts.

READERS:

There are 14 roles for readers, but if you do not have that many guests, you can always double or triple these roles, if needed.

PROP HOLDERS:

If you have Passover props, assign the plague props to all the children. When the Ten Plagues are mentioned, they can hold them up.

PASSOVER SEDER SCRIPT:
(It begins here)

NARRATOR:

Tonight begins Passover, but what exactly does that mean? From the outside looking in it seems like such a confusing holiday. First we eat this thing called Matzah that looks like a piece of cardboard. It pretty much tastes like cardboard too. The real madness happens when the darn thing gets hidden and all the kids are trying to find that one single piece called the Afikoman. Now before that, there is the strangest sight of all the grownups getting sloshed on these four cups of wine. For each glass they hold their bodies in a particular position, leaning to the left. Go figure!

But wait … there is still more to this thing called Passover! There are sounds of oohing coming from the guests, as items are pointed to on a big round plate. The oohing gets louder, when they get to actually taste the items and perhaps that is because everyone was waiting so long to be fed. Nevertheless, their tribal leader pushes forward and holds up each piece, and then shouts out words like, *"blood, fire and pillars of smoke"*, and then recites words in another language that appears not even the rest of the tribe understands. So, you can already see why Passover can be quite the confusing holiday. Even for us folks, who have been doing it for years, are still trying to figure out what it is all about.

Fortunately, those who participate in Passover have not lost their minds. If anything, they have only lost some sense of *"order"* in their lives and that is why they come together tonight to perform these strange rituals.

You see the word *"Seder"* actually means *"order"*. Order from what... you may ask? Well, how about all those chaotic emotions like doubt, anger, depression, fear, jealously, and judgment. Tonight begins the chance to escape all these road stopping feelings and start living the life we were all born to live! We will hear tonight the story of how the Israelites escaped from Egypt, but the most important lesson that we must take from this story is that we too do not have to be slaves to those chaotic emotions. They are our own personal Egypt. We too can achieve freedom. It all begins on how big our desire is to have it. So on that note, let us begin our Seder.

BLESSING OVER THE WINE

MAN OF THE HOUSE:
There will be four cups of wine we each will be drinking tonight. Yes four! Now while we are having all this fun, there is really a deeper meaning to what we will be doing here tonight. The four glasses of wine symbolize

four very important Hebrew letters that actually make up the highest level of God's name. It is called the Tetragrammaton; meaning having four letters. That is why we drink four glasses of wine.

There is also that leaning to the left movement we do every time we drink a glass. It is said that our selfish behavior enters in and out of the left side. When we lean to the left, it is crushing it. We then have the power, without interference, for the right side to do its job. The right side is positive energy that needs to be brought in to our lives, especially during Passover. It is recognized at this time of year how off balanced we all are. We have allowed too much of the left side to enter our lives and so the need to bring order and balance.

On that note, let us pour the first cup of wine. Lift your glass and let us all say the blessing over the first glass of wine, (of course, we will all lean to the left).

EVERYONE SAY:
Ba-ruch A-tah A-do-nai E-lo-hei-nu Me-lech Ha-o-lam, Bo-rei P'ri Ha-ga-fen.

MAN OF THE HOUSE:
Drink up!

WASHING OF THE HANDS

NARRATOR:
When we wash our hands, we are washing away any negativity. Since our hands are the busiest part of our body, they are the conductors that carry out negative deeds.

Our man of the house will pour a cup of water two times over the hands, starting with the left hand. (Let us pretend that he is doing this for everyone.) After he is done, let us all say the blessing below.

EVERYONE SAY:
Ba-ruch A-tah A-do-nai E-lo-hei-nu Me-lech Ha-o-

lam, A-sher Kid-sha-nu B'mitz-vo-tav V'tzi-va-nu

Aln'ti-lat Ya-dayim.

THE KARPUS

NARRATOR:

Karpus...Parsley...what does this green thing have to do with Passover? Well believe it or not, it can ignite the ability for us to gain control over our lives.

Wow, who knew Parsley could do all that? We are all going to have to go to Costco and buy the stuff in bulk!

No really ..., do you want to know where the real power is found in the Parsley? It is in the Hebrew letters that make up the word Parsley. It connects us on a diminutive level, much like atoms in a bomb. The Parsley has the power to wipe out our negativity in an instant, the same way one bomb can wipe out an entire city in an instant! That is the connection we are making here.

We are about to dip the "Parsley Bomb" into the salty water. No, we are not about to create an explosion here. We are only going to wipe out the tears and sweat from the Israelites who were slaves in Egypt. We will even wipe out our own tears and sweat that we have or might have in our lives. And imagine all that from a piece of Parsley!

Now our demonstrator will pick up a piece of Parsley. Let us all say the blessing below.

<u>BLESSING OF THE KARPUS</u>

<u>EVERYONE SAY:</u>
Ba-ruch A-tah A-do-nai E-lo-hei-nu Me-lech Ha-o-

lam, Bo-rei P'ri Ha-a-da-mah.

DIVIDING THE MATZAH

NARRATOR:

We are now at the part where we divide the Matzah. Now for those of you who do not know about this part, I am telling you, we divide the middle Matzah of the only three Matzah sitting on the table.

DEMONSTRATOR:

(Point to the three Matzah sitting on the table. Then pick up the middle Matzah and break it in half and hold them up for everyone to see.)

MAN OF THE HOUSE:

These two halves symbolize that half of our nature is negative and the other positive. The larger half, which is the positive half, is called the Afikoman. The positive half reminds us that we can create bigger results with our positive actions.

MAN OF THE HOUSE:

I will now take the Afikoman to be hidden later for the children to look for after the Passover meal.

THE FOUR QUESTIONS

MAN OF THE HOUSE:

I would like to ask all the children to stand up together and read the famous four questions out loud. All together now on the count of three … 1 … 2 … 3

1. **How is this night different from all other nights?**

2. **On all other nights, we may eat bread. Why on this night, do we only eat matzah?**

3. **On all other nights, we eat other kinds of herbs. Why on this night, we eat bitter herbs? On all other nights, we do not dip the herbs even once. Why on this night, do we dip them twice?**

4. **On all other nights, we eat sitting down. Why on this night, do we all recline?**

(The children all sit down afterwards.)

NARRATOR:

There is a part right about here, where we hear the very long story about these four men. There is a wise one, a wicked one, a simple one, and one that does not know how to ask. One does this and one does that, and for approximately 20 minutes we read about their whole story to learn a great lesson from it all. The man of the house will will give you the "Cliff Note" version.

MAN OF THE HOUSE

There is a wise man that goes all the way to seek the full meaning of Passover.

Then there is a wicked man that sees Passover as an event that we cannot change.

The next man is a simple man that sees that we were slaves, there was Moses and that he was a hero. The last of these men, is the one that does not know how to ask. He is a naïve man, who needs to be prompted with questions to initiate the desire to learn more.

NARRATOR:

Okay, did you all get it…? We will now be moving along to the Passover story.

THE PASSOVER STORY

READER 1:
Once upon a time…before *"He who shall not be named"* was around … there was another mean ole man who ruled all of Egypt. This man was called Pharaoh.

READER 2:
During this time in Egypt, Pharaoh used the Israelites as slaves to build Egypt's great cities. This went on for hundreds of years and for hundreds of years, they suffered under Pharaoh's rule.

READER 3:
One day Pharaoh declared that the first born male of the Hebrews were to be put to death. As we all know, because we have all seen the Cecil B Demille version of *The Ten Commandments*, that one very important first born male did not suffer the fate of Pharaoh's command.

READER 4:
Indeed we are talking about Moses! From the day he was drawn out from the Nile, his fate was destined. He was the greatest influencer Egypt had ever seen.

READER 5:

When Moses found out that he was Hebrew and began to embrace who he was, he started to see the pain and suffering of his people. Moses then felt that no man should be controlled, especially a slave. That was when things began to shift for the Israelites.

READER 6:

Of course that mean ole Pharaoh couldn't believe his ears when he heard that Moses was becoming a traitor to Egypt. This was unheard of, yet it was the truth. Moses was thrown out of Egypt because of that truth.

READER 7:

Moses walked with his wooded staff alone in the endless desert. Tired and thirsty … it was a matter of fate if he lived or died. If there truly was a God, then this God would lead Moses to wherever he needed to go.

READER 8:

And yes…Moses found out where he needed to go! He came upon that incredible burning bush, relaxed, took off his shoes, and hung out for awhile on that mountain top called Mount Sinai. Everything was really cool, until God instructed Moses to go back to Egypt and tell Pharaoh to, *"Let his people go!"*

READER 9:

Moses did what he was told to do because this was God you know. So with a few Godly tricks up his sleeve, Moses returned to Egypt. He stood before Pharaoh and said, *"Let my people go."* He did a bit of magic, but Pharaoh was not impressed. Pharaoh denied his wish and told Moses, *"You go back to your God."*

READER 10:

So Moses left. God realized that he had to be tougher on Pharaoh. Not to say he was a mean ole God, because you see, God loved Pharaoh too. It was just that Pharaoh had to be taught a lesson the hard way, since he was not willing to listen the easy way.

NARRATOR:

Let me interject here for a moment. How many of you can relate to learning a lesson the hard way? Can you recall a time when you thought, *"How could God be so mean to me?"* I believe we can all answer yes to that. The point to remember from this part of the story is that when challenges come to us in life, turn it around and look at it as a lesson of love from the Creator. It is his way of saying, *"I am here and I am showing you I am here, by putting you in front of your problem over and over again."* The bottom line is that he is telling us to change.

READER 11:

So...change had to happen for Pharaoh. God stepped in and brought those ten plagues to Egypt.

MAN OF THE HOUSE:

We will now pour the second cup of wine and lean to the left. Let us all say the blessing below.

EVERYONE SAY:

Ba-ruch A-tah A-do-nai E-lo-hei-nu Me-lech Ha-o-

lam, Bo-rei P'ri Ha-ga-fen.

MAN OF THE HOUSE:

Drink up.

THE PLAGUES

NARRATOR:

Ahh...now to the infamous ten plagues! Did you know they were actually separated into three groups? These three groups were the exact type of pain the Israelites went through. The first were the frogs and locust. They created terrible damage to the Egyptian land and homes. It made Pharaoh and his people slaves in the land where they lived.

Then there was the group of plagues that caused the Egyptians to suffer on their physical bodies. Yes, this is where the lice and boils come in. There was also darkness but it was not just that they could not see, their actual bodies were frozen in time and could not move.

Last, but not least, is the plague that stands alone. This is the one that caused the deepest pain. Yes ... this was the slaying of the first born. Sadly, God knew how to affect a man's soul, and this was the ultimate way to get Pharaoh to bend.

(Only to be read if kids have props Man of the house reads below.)
MAN OF THE HOUSE:
I would like all the children to stand with their props. When your plague is mentioned, please hold it up for everyone to see.

MAN OF THE HOUSE:
We are now going to do the strange act of dipping a finger into our wine cup and drip out three drops of wine onto our plate. We will then all say the words "Blood, Fire, Pillars of Smoke".

MAN OF THE HOUSE:
Is everyone ready? Let's all say together the words below...
EVERYONE SAY:
"Blood"..."Fire"..."Pillars of Smoke".

NARRATOR:

To make matters more confusing,
"Blood"..."Fire"...*"Pillars of Smoke"*...are also divided
into three groups. Let's hear what they are.

READER #12:

The first - blood, frogs, and lice represent the land and
sea turning against man. This was how he was hit from
below.

READER #13:

The second - beast, pest, and boils were how man got
hit at his own level.

READER #14:

The third - hail, locusts, and darkness hit man from
above.

NARRATOR:

We now see how all creation turned against the
Egyptians. It was the final plague that came from the
Creator himself, as the final destruction. However, as
we have heard year after year, that this was the
ultimate lesson.

MAN OF THE HOUSE:

Time for some more finger dipping! We will take ten
drops of wine with our finger and drip them onto our
plate. We then say the name of the 10 plagues.

EVERYONE SAY:
Frogs, Pests, Locusts, Lice, Boils, Beast, Hail, Blood, Darkness, Slaying of the First Born.

WASHING THE HANDS…AGAIN!

NARRATOR:
The Head of the House is now going to wash their hands in preparation for breaking the bread or, should we say, the Matzah.

HEAD OF HOUSE:
(Go to the water bowl and take hold of the pitcher, pour the water twice over the left hand, then twice over the right.)

HEAD OF HOUSE SAY:
Ba-ruch A-tah A-do-nai E-lo-hei-nu Me-lech Ha-o-lam, A-sher Kid-sha-nu B'mitz-vo-tav V'tzi-va-nu Al N'ti-lat Ya-da-yim.

NOW THE MATZAH!

NARRATOR:
Okay…about the Matzah! It is not a sponge, and it is not cardboard. The Matzah, believe it or not, is a

symbol for freedom. Now you may be wondering how this constipating stuff can symbolize freedom, but rest assure there is a good answer to this.

We have mentioned briefly before that we do not have to be "slaves" to our chaotic emotions. During this time of Passover, it is our chance to really escape our own personal Egypt. There is a cosmic window that opens up every year, for eight days during Passover. What that means is when the planets and moon align in a certain way, and at the same time every year, it creates an energy, or let us say; a mood inside us. It is the same kind of cosmic energy that the moon uses to affect the way the tides move. So…if one moon can move one ocean, imagine how it can move our tiny bodies that are made up of 85% water!

Okay…so you probably want to know how any of this has to do with the Matzah. Well, in order to have freedom from the emotions that keep us trapped, we have to find a way to set them aside; restrict ourselves from letting them swell up inside us. It is like when we want to make homemade bread. We add the yeast to make the bread rise, but if we did not put the yeast in, then the bread would not rise at all. Eating Matzah, instead of the bread, is a form of restriction, and that restriction keeps us from letting our chaotic emotions rise within us. The eating of the Matzah is a way of showing our desire to be free. That is the connection we are making here tonight. During the eight days, this cosmic window is opened. It gives us that extra boost in order to bring the order we are trying to achieve during this time of Passover. The more we restrict, the better our chance of really being free.

MAN OF THE HOUSE:
We are now going to recite the blessing over the Matzah.
DEMONSTRATOR:
(Lift the Matzah and hold it up for everyone to see.)

EVERYONE SAY:
Ba-ruch A-tah A-do-nai E-lo-hei-nu Me-lech Ha-o-lam, Ha-mo-tzi Le-chem Hin Ha-a-retz. Ba-ruch A-tah A-do-nai E-lo-hei-nu Me-lech Ha-o-lam, A-sher Kid-sha-nu B'mitz-vo-tav V'tzi-va-nu Al A-chee-la Ma-tzah.

MAN OF THE HOUSE:
You may eat the Matzah.

THE SEDER PLATE

NARRATOR:
Ah yes .... This wonderful Seder plate! What is it with these things on it that make them so special? Well, for

starters, since we can not see spiritual energy or the compulsion's that push them to work, we rely on more visible objects to help us relate to them and that way we can connect to them. You see, during Passover the items on the plate become embodied with an energy that stems from the Tree of Life.

This injects us with energy to make our lives easier. Oh boy, did that one go over everybody's head? Okay, let me explain it like this...imagine the Tree of Life being an elevator in the department store called *GET YOUR LIFE.* All you have to do is go to each floor and take what you need. With that said, we will begin to take a closer look at what is really meant by all those things on that Seder plate. So hang tight! We are about to go on the Seder plate elevator ride and get what we need in our lives. Here we go!

DEMONSTRATOR:
(Point to the Matzah.)

MAN OF THE HOUSE:
The three Matzah represent the highest levels of the Tree of Life that symbolize balance. It is like the top floor of the department store. Achieving balance in our life is similar to how a light bulb works. There are three components inside the light bulb. There is the positive wire, the negative wire, and the filament. The filament balances the two energy wires. This creates the circuit of continuity for the light to stay on. We are also trying to keep our own light on. We achieve this by keeping

the filament inside us intact and not letting the energies we have overpower us and cause short circuits. That is why Balance is the top floor.

DEMONSTRATOR:
(Point to the Shank Bone.)

MAN OF THE HOUSE:
The Shank Bone represents a couple of things. First, because it is from the meat of an animal, it signifies sacrifice. It is also the level on the Tree of Life, or should we say, the department floor level, that we see how to really share with others. But in order to really share ourselves, we must set aside what we want, in a way that can sometimes feel like a sacrifice. That is the connection to the Shank Bone.

DEMONSTRATOR:
(Point to the Egg.)

NARRATOR:
The Egg assumes the role of a couple of things. The first it stands for the nation of Israel, because for the Israelites it was the new beginning. Second the more we cook an egg, the harder it gets. We are all like that overcooked egg. The harder we hold onto our own belief systems and the harder we disagree with others, the harder we become. The elevator door opens us up to a level of breaking this pattern. It softens us to the people that we do not relate to. That is why we roast

the Egg until it cracks. We are all way overcooked. We should all acknowledge this, so we can crack and accept opposing views. The best part is it might even serve for the common good. That is the connection to the Egg.

DEMONSTRATOR:
(Point to the Maror/Horseradish.)

NARRATOR:
When we eat from the bitter Herbs, we find it is pretty brutal on the taste buds. We are therefore making a rather quick acknowledgement to what those Israelites went through the moment that Maror hits our tongue.

Sometimes we need a harsh reality to happen in our lives, to wake us up and get us back on track. When we are faced with these truths, we begin to see truth, and we are able to hang on to that force that is pushing us to change and create balance. The elevator door here opens up to the floor of understanding. We learn that here in the world, exists an energy of balance and sometimes it is hard to see.

We are now about to do two things: say the blessing over the Maror and then subject ourselves to eating as much as we can of this stuff. Now remember, this stuff can be quite harsh. Some may get tears in their eyes, some may cough, and some might get that gag reflex thing going on. Some might have to call 911 and some will act like it is no big deal. The idea here is to physically break our limitations of what we think we can tolerate. When each of us does that, we are making a connection to a force that has the ability to shorten the process of any harsh challenges we may be going through. Even as we all sit here together as a group, we are creating an opening for others on a global level.

MAN OF THE HOUSE:
Please take some Maror and Matzah and make a sandwich. Let us all say the blessing below.

EVERYONE SAY:
Ba-ruch A-tah A-do-nai E-lo-hei-nu Me-lech Ha-o-

lam, A-sher Kid-sha-nu B'mitz-vo-tav V'tzi-va-nu Al

A-chee-las Maw-ror.

DEMONSRATOR:
(Point to the Charosets.)

NARRATOR:
The Charosets taste sweet. The sweetness helps to counteract any shameful or terrible past thing we might have done. So take as much as you like because when this elevator door opens, we are able to make that commitment to do things differently. Let us all say the blessing below.

EVERYONE SAY:
Ba-ruch A-tah A-do-nai E-lo-hei-nu Me-lech Ha-o-lam, A-sher Kid-sha-nu B'mitz-vo-tav V'tzi-va-nu Cha-ro-sets.

DEMONSTRATOR:
(Point to the Karpus/Parsley.)

NARRATOR:
Just to recap. The Karpus is that "Parsley Bomb" stuff that has the power to wipe out all our negativity. Let us all say the blessing below.

EVERYONE SAY:
Ba-ruch A-tah A-do-nai E-lo-hei-nu Me-lech Ha-o-lam, bor-rei pe-ri ha-a-da-ma.

DEMONSTRATOR:
(Point to the Chazeret/Lettuce.)

NARRATOR:
The Chazeret symbolizes a collection center for all our negative acts. It combines it all together like a trash can collects all our garbage. This allows the trash truck to come by and remove the trash all at once. When the elevator door opens here, we are able to get rid of our negativity in a single shot. Let us all say the blessing below.

EVERYONE SAY:
Ba-ruch A-tah A-do-nai E-lo-hei-nu Me-lech Ha-o-lam, bor-rei pe-ri ha-etz.

MAN OF THE HOUSE:
We are now ready to eat our Seder meal and we will conclude our Seder after we have filled our stomach with all the delicious foods that were made here tonight!
(Man of the house should hide the Afikoman at this time).

AFTER THE MEAL

MAN OF THE HOUSE:
I would like to ask all the children to get up because it is now time to look for the Afikoman.

(Allow enough time for the children to find the Afikoman. Once it is found, break it into as many pieces as you have guests, and share these pieces with them to eat.)

MAN OF THE HOUSE:
Let us all say the blessing after the meal.

EVERYONE SAY:
Baruch ata Adonoy, Eloheinu melech ha-olam, ha-zan es ha-olam kulo be-tuvo

be-chein be-chesed uve-rachamim hu nosein lechem le-chol basar, ki le-olam chasdo. Uv-tuvo ha-gadol, tamid lo chasar lanu ve'al yechsar lanu mazon le-olam va'ed. Ba'avur shemo ha gadol ki hu El zan umi-farneis la-kol u-meitiv la-kol u-meichin mazon le-chol beriyosav asher bara. Baruch ata Adonoy, ha-zan es ha-kol.

MAN OF THE HOUSE:
We are now going to pour the third cup of wine and welcome the prophet Elijah. Let us all say the blessing below.

EVERYONE SAY:
Ba-ruch A-tah A-do-nai E-lo-hei-nu Me-lech Ha-o-

lam, Bo-rei P'ri Ha-ga-fen.

EVERYONE DO:
Drink while leaning to the left.

NARRATOR:
There is a part here where everyone starts singing a bunch of Passover songs. If anyone would like to do this feel free to begin singing.
(If no one begins to sing then say, *"Moving along then"*).

MAN OF THE HOUSE:

Finally we are at the fourth cup of wine! Please pour the fourth cup of wine, and together. Let us all say the blessing below.

EVERYONE SAY:

Ba-ruch A-tah A-do-nai E-lo-hei-nu Me-lech Ha-o-lam, Bo-rei P'ri Ha-ga-fen.

EVERYONE DO:

Drink while leaning to the left.

NARRATOR:

Now that you are all had plenty of wine and cannot help leaning to the left, and then the right, and then back to the left again, I think you are all ready to hear the 20 minute version about the wise man, the wicked man, the simple man, and the one that does not know how to ask. Oh …. Just kidding! I'm only playing around here with all of you. We are actually done with our Seder and I hope you all enjoyed it. So with that said…let us all make this time an opportunity for all of us to break free. Freedom is just a parting sea away. If it happened once before, then, why would it not happen again?

THE END

About the Author: Lisa Benger was raised Los Angeles California, in a reform Jewish home. In her twenties she studied some Orthodox Judaism that later led her to the teachings of Kabbalah. This was the spark that inspired her to put into simple words, the meaning of all the Jewish holidays. The Painless Passover is the first of her spiritual books to be published. There are more to come!

Lisa Benger resides in Scottsdale Arizona now with her son Jakob.

Website: youngcreateers.com – Get on the mailing list to learn about the newest releases and other books written by Lisa Benger!

Made in the USA
Lexington, KY
17 February 2017